Sweet

[CAST IRON]

CREATIONS

Sweet CAST IRON CREATIONS

dutch oven desserts

Hobble Creek Press

An imprint of Cedar Fort, Inc.

Springville, Utah

DOUG MARTIN

ISBN 13: 978-1-4621-1445-0

Published by Hobble Creek Press, an imprint of Cedar Fort, Inc.
2373 W. 700 S., Springville, UT, 84663
Distributed by Cedar Fort, Inc., www.cedarfort.com

Library of Congress Cataloging-in-Publication Data

Martin, Doug, 1970-
Sweet cast iron creations / Doug Martin.
 pages cm
Includes index.
ISBN 978-1-4621-1445-0 (acid-free paper)
1. Dutch oven cooking. 2. Desserts. I Title.

TX840.D88M37 2014
641.5'89--dc23

2014031138

Cover and page design by Bekah Claussen
Cover design © 2015 Lyle Mortimer
Edited by Justin Greer

Printed in the United States of America

10 9 8 7 6 5 4 3 2 1

Printed on acid-free paper

There are a few people I would like to thank for making this book possible. First off, I would like to thank my mom and grandmothers for instilling the love of cooking in me from an early age. Watching my grandmothers bake apple pies or all of the cookies they used to spoil me with, or seeing how my mom could stretch one pound of meat into something that tasted great and could feed a family of seven, started me down the road to becoming the cook that I am today. I would also like to thank T, who got me started in competitive cooking, and my cooking partner, Matt Pelton, who really helped shrink the Dutch oven learning curve. And last, but certainly not least, I would like to thank my wife, Racheall, for all of her help and for putting up with all the scattered Dutch ovens in the kitchen while I worked on all the recipes. I could not have done this without her.

CONTENTS

SWEET ROLLS AND DESSERT BREADS

FROSTINGS, GANACHES, AND COMPOTES

CHOOSING YOUR CAST IRON

When choosing what type of cast iron you will need, there are a few things you should consider. Are you going to use them at home or in the field? What size Dutch oven or skillet do you need to meet your needs? Would you rather use vintage or new cast iron?

I prefer to use vintage cast iron. It is a lot lighter and smoother than the cast iron you can buy in the store today. I will hit up the antiques mall or garage sales on the weekends to find the ones I use. You can usually get them for a good price as well. Most of the ones you will find will have years of seasoning built up on them, but with a little elbow grease they can be cleaned and will give you a lifetime of use. When buying cast iron like this, there are a few things you should look for. You should set the piece down on a flat surface to make sure that it is not warped or what is called a spinner. When set on a flat surface, the warped ones will spin like a top. This will not work well on a stove, but would still work okay over a campfire. Another thing you should check is if it has any cracks or chips. Sometimes you will not be able to see them because of the buildup on the pan or Dutch oven. If you hold the pan up and thump it, it should sound like you are ringing a bell. After checking all this and purchasing your vintage cast iron, you can follow the instructions in chapter 2 to get your cast iron ready to cook in.

If you do not want to go searching for vintage cast iron, you can find many fine new products for sale. They can be found at most outdoor stores and are generally already seasoned and ready for you to use.

The next thing to consider is where you are going to use your cast iron. A variety of different Dutch ovens can be used indoors or outdoors. The Dutch ovens for camping will have three legs on the bottom and a lip around the top to keep the charcoal from falling off. The indoor Dutch ovens will not have the legs, and the lids will be rounded and without the lip. If you have a gas stove, you can use the outdoor ovens indoors as well by placing the legs down through the grate.

Now that you have decided which style of oven you will need, it's time to decide on the size. For most jobs, the 10- and 12-inch Dutch ovens should be adequate. When you get up to the 14- and 16-inch ovens, you have to keep weight in mind. A 14-inch Dutch oven will weigh around 22 pounds when empty. After you have cooked your meal, you could be at 25 to 28 pounds, and that is a lot of weight to move around. I prefer to use two 12-inch Dutch ovens. A 12-inch Dutch oven is good for 10 to 15 servings, depending on what you are cooking.

STRIPPING, SEASONING, CLEANING, AND STORAGE OF CAST IRON

STRIPPING

Many myths are out there about how to properly care for your Dutch ovens and various pieces of cast iron. In this chapter, I show you the best way to strip, season, and care for your cast iron so that it will last and can be passed down through the generations.

I really enjoy hunting for vintage cast iron, and I highly recommend it. It has a much smoother surface and is generally lighter than the cast iron produced today. The only trouble is that most of the pieces you find will be covered with layer after layer of seasoning that has built up over years of use, and you need to strip this off.

You can strip the piece using a couple of methods. My favorite method for restoring a vintage piece is by using electrolysis. You will need a plastic container to do this; I use a 5-gallon bucket for the smaller pieces and a rubber tote for the larger pieces. You will also need a battery charger that has a manual mode. If it only has the automatic mode, it will not work. You will also need a piece of steel. I use a small piece of expanded metal. To hang the piece I use an S-hook and suspend it from a wooden dowel. The last thing that is needed is the electrolyte. For this I use Arm & Hammer All Natural Super Washing Soda. Make sure to do this outside.

To set up, fill your bucket or tub with water, leaving enough room at the top so that it will not overflow when the cast iron is added. Use 1 tablespoon of the washing soda per gallon of water. Take your piece of steel and secure it to the side of the bucket or tub. Next, place the wooden dowel across the bucket or tub with the S-hook on it. Then hang your piece of cast iron from the hook, making sure it does not touch the steel. At this point, put the positive lead to the piece of steel and the negative lead to the cast iron. Now plug in the battery charger. You should see bubbles start coming to the surface. This will remove the rust from old pieces and will loosen the built-up seasoning from the pan. The length of time will depend on the charger. The higher the amps, the quicker it will strip the piece. After a few hours, unplug the charger and remove the piece. I like to scrub it with steel wool to remove all the loose pieces. If everything has not come off, just return it to the tank and repeat until the piece has been stripped to bare metal.

SEASONING

Now it is time to season your Dutch oven or other cast iron. Whether you are seasoning a newly stripped piece or a piece that you just purchased, it will be the same.

Most new pieces that you purchase today will come seasoned and ready to use, but you can add another coat to help build up the nonstick surface.

There are different ways to season your cast iron. If you want to think about your family's safety, you can do it in the house in your oven. This method will test your smoke detectors and make sure they are functioning properly.

You can also do it over a camp stove or BBQ grill outside so you don't smoke everyone out. I don't recommend using a campfire. The heat of the fire is too hot and can damage your cast iron. It can cause it to warp and can also change the properties of the cast iron. You can tell when this happens because the Dutch oven will have a reddish tint to it that is not rust. When this happens, you will not be able to season it properly.

My method of choice is to use the oven. To do this, first wash out the Dutch oven and then make sure it is completely dry. I dry it by putting it on the burner of the stove. Once it is dry, let it cool until you can handle it, and then coat it with a light layer of oil. I prefer to use Crisco or lard; both work well. You can also use canola or vegetable oil as well.

I then preheat my oven to 450 degrees and place the piece into the oven as it is heating up, with the opening of the Dutch oven or skillet facing down. I do this because as the pan heats up, the oil will vaporize. If the opening is up, you will be seasoning the top of your oven rather than your cooking surface. After about 15 minutes, using a pot holder, remove the pan and wipe it out to remove the excess oil. Then place the piece back into the oven and continue to bake it for about an hour and a half. By this time it should have stopped smoking. Turn off the oven and let the piece cool down in the oven. Once it is cools, it is ready to use. You can add as many coats as you think are necessary to get the cooking surface to the point you want it.

CLEANING AND STORAGE

Here is where some of the myths come in. Some people think that you cannot use dish soap on cast iron. I always use soap on my cast iron. When I go to cook a chocolate cake, I don't want it to taste like the lasagna I cooked the day before.

The thing to remember is to only use a drop or two of dish soap because it is ultra-concentrated. First, use a plastic scraper to remove the large pieces of leftover food. Then add warm water and a drop of dish soap and wash it out with a plastic scrub brush. Rinse it well and give it the smell test to make sure you cannot smell the soap. Finally, dry it on the stovetop burner until all the water has evaporated.

Now it is time to store your cast iron. At this point, most people I know would put a light coat of oil on their Dutch oven. I don't recommend this. I always put my cast iron away dry. I do this because if you are storing your cast iron for long periods of time, the oil will go rancid. When the oil goes rancid, it becomes acidic, and it will eat away at that nice nonstick surface you have worked so hard to create. So I recommend storing your Dutch ovens dry. When it is time to cook, then you can put your coat of oil on it and get straight to creating all those amazing dishes.

INTRODUCTION **3**

CAST IRON COOKING METHODS

Cooking in cast iron, for me, is the only way to cook. I have given away all of my stainless steel pots and pans and now cook everything in cast iron. I have found that food always turns out better when I cook in cast iron.

Before I started cooking in Dutch ovens, I was a little intimidated. Everyone I talked to would tell me that it was difficult to do and that they would burn things a lot. I have found things to be just the opposite. Not only is cooking in cast iron not complicated, but it is also a lot of fun. When you go camping with your friends and family, you can impress them with the amazing food you can create with just a black pot and some charcoal.

First, cast iron cooking gives you very even heat. If you put a stainless steel pan on an electric stove, you can see the pattern of the heating element show up on the pan; the steel does not distribute the heat as well. Put a cast iron pan on the same stove, and you will not have that problem, because the cast iron distributes the heat evenly. One way to see this is to put a wet cast iron pan on the stove and turn on the heat. You can watch how fast the heat spreads evenly through the pan as the water evaporates.

Cooking in cast iron also has health benefits. For example, when you cook in a Dutch oven or skillet, some of the iron leaches into your food, which can help people who are anemic.

There are four main types of Dutch oven cooking: baking, roasting, broiling, and braising. I will cover all types of cooking and how to set up the coals to do so, but for this book, we will be primarily using the baking method.

BAKING

Baking is used for breads and desserts. It's also where many people have the most trouble. I see a lot of breads that are cooked nicely on top but burned on the bottom. I have never burned the bottoms using the following baking style; the bread turns out a nice golden brown.

First, place a ring of charcoal around the bottom of your Dutch oven, spacing them 1 to 1½ inches apart. The important thing is to put the coal only halfway under the oven, leaving half of the coal exposed. This way, the heat will go up the side of the pot, and then the air will be heated under the Dutch oven. You will not have hotspots underneath to cause burning.

For the top of the Dutch oven, place another ring of charcoal around the outside of the lid, also spaced 1 to 1½ inches apart. Then, use what we call a checkerboard pattern. In this case, I am using a 10-inch Dutch oven, so I have placed 1 coal on either side of the handle. On a 12-inch Dutch oven, where you have more surface area, I would move the 2 center coals to the side a little and add 2 more coals in the middle.

TOP    BOTTOM

ROASTING

The next type of cooking is roasting. This is used for cooking chicken, roasts, and other types of meats and potatoes that you would make for a main dish. For this method, place the coal opposite from what we did for baking. Put a single ring of lit coals on the top of the Dutch oven, spaced 1 to 1½ inches apart. On the bottom, put a ring of coals around the outside and use the checkerboard of coals in the middle.

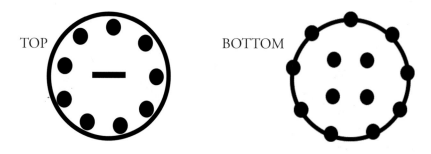

BRAISING

The third type of cooking you can do in your Dutch oven is braising. This type of cooking can be used for braising meats and vegetables and for making soups, stews, and chilies. In this type of cooking, you want all of your heat on the bottom, so do not put any coals on the top lid. When you are making chili, the beans will float to the surface. If you have coals on the top, you will burn your beans. For this type of cooking, use the ring of coals and the checkerboard under your Dutch oven and nothing on top.

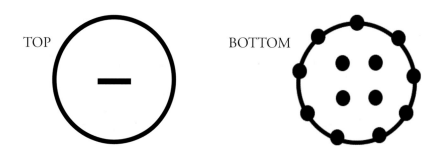

BROILING

The final type of cooking is broiling. It is probably the least used out of all of the cooking methods. For this type of cooking, you will want all of your heat on the top and nothing on the bottom. For outdoor cooking, I mainly use this method to finish dishes. If you have roasted a chicken and want to crisp up the skin, remove all the heat from the bottom and place the coals on top. This way, you will not burn the bottom, and the skin will be nice and crispy—very different from the colorless and rubbery skin that you get without broiling it.

TOP    BOTTOM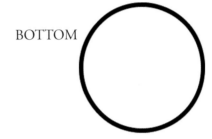

PIES

FLAKY PIE CRUST

My wife has used this recipe since she was about 12 years old. I came across it one day and tried it out, and now it is the standard for all of my pie recipes. Nothing beats a great homemade flaky pie crust filled with your favorite fillings. This recipe makes two crusts.

2½ cups flour
1 tsp. salt
1 cup butter, cut into cubes
1 egg, beaten
1 Tbsp. vinegar
¼ cup cold water

1. Mix flour and salt in a medium-sized bowl. Using a pastry cutter, cut the butter into the flour until it is pea sized. In a separate bowl, mix the beaten egg, vinegar, and cold water. Add the liquid mixture to the flour mixture and mix together until it forms a ball. Only knead the dough enough to form a ball.

2. Working on a clean, floured surface, roll out the dough to a ⅝-inch thickness. Lightly flour the rolled-out dough and fold in half. Lightly flour the half and fold into a quarter. Pick up and place the point of the dough in the center of your pan and unfold. Gently work the dough into the corners of the pan. Refrigerate dough 15–20 minutes before filling.

HOT APPLE PIE

I have made many apple pies throughout the years, and I finally came up with a great recipe that, if combined with my Flaky Pie Crust recipe, makes for a delicious dessert. I like my apples to still have a little crunch to them and not to be mushy, so I don't pre-cook them.

1 pre-made Flaky Pie Crust
3–4 lb. apples, peeled, cored, and sliced
Juice of 1 lemon
3/4 cup sugar
3/4 cup light brown sugar
1 tsp. cinnamon
1/2 tsp. nutmeg
2 Tbsp. cornstarch
1 beaten egg (for brushing on top crust)

Place peeled, cored, and sliced apples in a large bowl and cover with the juice of 1 lemon. Toss to coat—this keeps the apples from browning. Add sugar, brown sugar, cinnamon, nutmeg, and flour to apples. Place crust in oiled 10-inch Dutch oven. Mix well the apples and place in the crust. Cover with second crust or lattice top. Take beaten egg and brush on top crust, covering the whole crust. Bake (using the baking method found in Chapter 3) for 1 hour or until crust is golden brown.

CHEESECAKE BROWNIE PIE

Combining two of my wife's favorite desserts was a big hit. You will partially bake the brownie crust before adding the cheesecake filling. If you don't, your cheesecake will sink through the brownie batter and it will be more like a cheesy brownie.

For the brownie crust:
1/2 cup butter
2 oz. semi-sweet chocolate chips
2 large eggs
1 cup sugar
1 tsp. vanilla extract
3/4 cup flour

For the cheesecake filling:
2 (8-oz.) pkgs. cream cheese
1/2 cup sugar
2 large eggs
1/2 tsp. vanilla extract

BROWNIE CRUST

1. Melt the butter and chocolate chips over low heat, using just enough coals to melt them. Add the remaining ingredients. Mix well. Pour into a greased 10-inch Dutch oven. Place coals (according to the baking method found in Chapter 3). Bake for 12–15 minutes, until the crust has just set up. Remove from the heat.

CHEESECAKE FILLING

2. Cream the cream cheese and sugar. Add the eggs and vanilla extract. Mix until smooth. Pour over the pre-cooked brownie crust and smooth out as needed. Return to heat (following the baking pattern found in Chapter 3). Bake for 20–35 minutes, until a toothpick inserted in the center comes out clean.

3. Let cool and chill for several hours. Best served chilled.

THERESA'S CARAMEL APPLE PIE

If you like caramel apples, then you will enjoy this pie. This is a delicious pie from one of my mom's friends. She won first place in the Iowa State Fair with this one.

For the crust:
12–15 graham crackers, finely crushed
1/4 cup sugar
7 Tbsp. melted butter

For the topping:
1/4 cup sugar
1 (8-oz.) pkg. cream cheese, softened
1 (8-oz.) container Cool Whip

For the filling:
6–8 Fuji apples, peeled, cored, and sliced
1 (3-oz.) box lemon-flavored gelatin
2 tsp. cinnamon
1/4 tsp. coriander (optional)
1 (3-oz.) box vanilla cook-and-serve pudding
1 jar caramel sauce

1. In a 12-inch Dutch oven, combine the apples, half of the water called for on the lemon gelatin box, lemon gelatin, cinnamon, and coriander (if desired). Cook using the braising method found in Chapter 3 until the apples are tender. Add the vanilla pudding with 1–2 tablespoons of water, just enough to dissolve the pudding. Bring to a rolling boil. Remove from heat and let cool.

2. While the filling is cooling, make the graham cracker crust by combining ingredients. Press into a 10-inch Dutch oven and pour half the jar of caramel sauce over the crust. Set aside.

3. For the topping, cream the sugar and cream cheese until fluffy. Fold into the Cool Whip. Pour the cooled apple filling mixture into the crust and top with the topping. Drizzle remaining caramel sauce over the top.

GREEN CHILI APPLE PIE

I came up with this twist on apple pie for a contest I entered. A lot of people will wrinkle their noses at the idea of green chili in an apple pie, but it gives it a nice spicy twist. We eat a lot of green chili in my home, because my wife and her family are Hispanic. Before I met my wife, I had never really had green chili. Her family introduced me to new foods and gave me the idea to add green chili to other dishes. For the bottom crust, you will use the Flaky Pie Crust recipe.

1 pre-made Flaky Pie Crust

For the filling:
3–4 lb. apples, peeled, cored, and sliced
Juice of 1 lime
$^3/_4$ cup sugar
$^3/_4$ cup brown sugar
$^1/_4$ cup green chili, roasted, peeled, and seeded
1 tsp. cinnamon
$^1/_4$ tsp. nutmeg
3 Tbsp. cornstarch

For the topping:
1 cup quick oats
$^1/_2$ cup flour
$^1/_2$ tsp. cinnamon
$^1/_8$ tsp. nutmeg
$^1/_2$ cup sugar
$^1/_2$ cup crispy chopped bacon
1 cup mild cheddar cheese, shredded
1 cup butter, melted

1. Place crust in 10-inch Dutch oven.
2. In large bowl, cover apples with lime juice. Toss to coat—this keeps apples from browning. Add remaining filling ingredients to apples. Mix well and place in pie crust.
3. In medium bowl, mix oats, flour, cinnamon, nutmeg, sugar, and bacon. Add melted butter and mix. Add shredded cheese and mix. Crumble over pie filling and bake (using baking method found in Chapter 3) for 1 hour.

BUTTERMILK PIE

1 pre-made Flaky Pie Crust
1½ cups sugar
1 Tbsp. flour
4 eggs
½ cup butter, melted
1 cup buttermilk
1 tsp. vanilla extract

In a medium bowl, stir together the sugar and flour. Whisk in the eggs one at a time. Add the melted butter, buttermilk, and vanilla extract. Mix well. Place pie crust in an oiled 10-inch Dutch oven. Pour into pie crust and bake (using baking method found in Chapter 3). Bake for 60 minutes or until the top is lightly browned and the center has set. Cool and serve at room temperature.

SWEET POTATO CRUNCH PIE

This is a great alternative to pumpkin pie. I first introduced this at our family Thanksgiving, and there wasn't a slice left afterward. My neighbor's children actually request this pie throughout the year. It is very velvety and smooth. The toffee in the topping adds a delightful crunch.

1 pre-made Flaky Pie Crust

Filling
³/₄ cup sugar
¹/₂ tsp. salt
1 tsp. cinnamon
¹/₂ tsp. ground ginger
¹/₄ tsp. ground cloves
2 eggs
15 oz. puréed sweet potato
1 (12-oz.) can evaporated milk

Topping
1 cup quick oats
¹/₂ cup flour
¹/₂ cup sugar
¹/₂ tsp. cinnamon
¹/₂ cup butter, melted
1 cup Heath toffee bits without chocolate

1. In a small bowl, stir together sugar, salt, cinnamon, ginger, and cloves. In a large bowl, beat eggs. Add the sugar and spice mixture into the eggs and mix together. Mix in the puréed sweet potatoes. Add evaporated milk and mix until well blended. Place pie crust in an oiled 10-inch Dutch oven. Pour the mixture into pie crust and bake (using baking method found in Chapter 3) for 45–55 minutes (until a probe inserted into the center comes out clean).

2. While the pie is baking, mix all the topping ingredients together. When the pie is done, spread the topping onto the top of the pie and broil (using broiling method found in Chapter 3) for an additional 15 minutes. Cool and serve.

TURTLE PIE

This twist on a classic pecan pie is delicious, especially for chocolate lovers. I came up with this one for Thanksgiving, and it was one of the first pies to disappear.

1 pre-made Flaky Pie Crust
1 cup light corn syrup
$^3/_4$ cup sugar
$^1/_3$ cup butter
$^1/_2$ cup semi-sweet chocolate chips
4 eggs, beaten
1 tsp. maple extract
$1^1/_2$ cups pecan halves

1. In a small Dutch oven, combine corn syrup, sugar, and butter. Heat using the braising coal placement found in Chapter 3. Cook until sugar dissolves and butter melts. Remove from coals and add chocolate chips and stir until completely melted. Cool slightly (otherwise, when you add your eggs, they will cook upon contact). Add beaten eggs slowly while mixing. Add maple extract and combine well. Stir in pecan halves.

2. Line 10-inch Dutch oven with pie crust and pour filling into crust. Bake (using the baking method found in Chapter 3) for 55–60 minutes. Pie is done when probe inserted near center comes out clean. Remove from heat; cool completely before serving.

BLACKBERRY RHUBARB PIE

I've always loved strawberry rhubarb pie, so one day I thought I would experiment with other berries, and this is what I came up with. My wife, who hates rhubarb, loved this pie.

1 pre-made Flaky Pie Crust
12 oz. blackberries
¼ lb. rhubarb, peeled and cut into 1-inch pieces
¾ cup brown sugar
1 cup sugar
⅛ tsp. ground nutmeg
3 Tbsp. lime juice
3 Tbsp. cornstarch

1. In a 10-inch Dutch oven, mix blackberries, rhubarb, sugars, nutmeg, and lime juice. Use the braising method found in Chapter 3, and bring the mixture to a boil. Add cornstarch and boil for 1 minute. Remove from heat and set aside.

2. Roll out half of the pre-made crust dough and place in the bottom of a 10-inch Dutch oven. Pour in the fruit filling and spread it evenly around the crust. Roll out the remaining half of the dough and place on top of the filling. Pinch the top and bottom crusts together around the edges. Cut a few slits on the top (for ventilation). Use the baking method from Chapter 3 and cook for 40–45 minutes or until golden brown. Let pie cool before serving so that the fruit juices set up.

MANGO CHERRY PIE

1 pre-made Flaky Pie Crust
1 (30-oz.) can cherry pie filling
1½ cups fresh mango, diced
1 Tbsp. lime juice

In a large bowl, mix cherry pie filling, mango, and lime juice. Set aside. Roll out half of the pre-made crust dough and place in the bottom of a 10-inch Dutch oven. Pour in the fruit filling and spread it evenly around the crust. Roll out the remaining half of the dough and place it on top of the filling. Pinch the top and bottom crusts together around the edges. Cut a few slits on the top (for ventilation). Use the baking method from Chapter 3 and cook for 40–45 minutes or until golden brown. Let pie cool before serving so that the fruit juices set up.

"BLACK AND BLUE" BERRY PIE

1 pre-made Flaky Pie Crust
2 (6-oz.) pkgs. fresh blueberries
2 (6-oz.) pkgs. fresh blackberries
¾ cup brown sugar
¾ cup sugar
¼ cup water
1 tsp. raspberry extract
2 Tbsp. lime juice
3 Tbsp. cornstarch

1. In a 10-inch Dutch oven, combine berries, sugars, water, raspberry extract, and lime juice. Use the braising method found in Chapter 3 and bring the mixture to a boil. Add cornstarch and boil for 1 minute. Remove from heat and set aside.

2. Roll out half of the pre-made crust dough and place in the bottom of a 10-inch Dutch oven. Pour in the fruit filling and spread it evenly around the crust. Roll out the remaining half of the dough and place on top of the filling. Pinch the top and bottom crusts together around the edges. Cut a few slits on the top (for ventilation). Use the baking method from Chapter 3 and cook for 40–45 minutes or until golden brown. Let pie cool before serving so that the fruit juices set up.

OLD-FASHIONED PECAN PIE

1 pre-made Flaky Pie Crust
1 cup light corn syrup
³/₄ cup sugar
¹/₃ cup butter
4 eggs, beaten
1 tsp. vanilla extract
1¹/₂ cups pecan halves

1. In small Dutch oven, combine corn syrup, sugar, and butter. Heat using the braising coal placement found in Chapter 3. Cook until sugar dissolves and butter melts. Remove from coals. Cool slightly (otherwise, when you add the eggs, they will cook upon contact). Add beaten eggs slowly while mixing. Add vanilla extract and combine well. Stir in pecan halves.

2. Line 10-inch Dutch oven with pie crust; pour filling into crust. Bake (using baking method found in Chapter 3) for 55–60 minutes. Pie is done when probe inserted near center comes out clean. Remove from heat and cool completely before serving.

RASPBERRY CHERRY PIE

This is one of my favorite pies. I like to use fresh fruit and pit the cherries myself, but you can also use frozen fruit. The tartness of the fruit is rounded out by the sugars.

1 pre-made Flaky Pie Crust
2 cups raspberries
2 cups cherries, pitted
3/4 cup brown sugar
3/4 cup sugar
2 Tbsp. lime juice
3 Tbsp. cornstarch

Combine the raspberries, cherries, sugars, lime juice, and cornstarch, and then set aside. Roll out pie crust and place in the bottom of an oiled 10-inch Dutch oven. Pour pie filling in the crust and spread evenly. Cover with the second crust. Cut slits in the top to release steam. Bake (using the baking method in Chapter 3) for 40–50 minutes or until crust is golden brown. Let cool before serving.

TRIPLE BERRY PIE

This was my late sister-in-law's favorite pie. The combination of berries has the right amount of tartness and sweetness. I use frozen berries, but you can use fresh.

1 pre-made Flaky Pie Crust
2 cups raspberries
2 cups blackberries
1 cup blueberries
¾ cup brown sugar
¾ cup sugar
¼ tsp. nutmeg
2 Tbsp. lime juice
3 Tbsp. cornstarch

Combine the raspberries, blackberries, blueberries, sugars, nutmeg, lime juice, and cornstarch and set aside. Roll out pie crust and place in bottom of oiled 10-inch Dutch oven. Pour pie filling in crust and spread evenly. Cover with second crust. Cut slits in the top to release steam. Bake (using the baking method in Chapter 3) for 40–50 minutes or until crust is golden brown. Let cool before serving.

CAKES

During the years I have been experimenting with cake recipes, I have found a few secrets that will help you have moist cakes that don't stick to the pan. The first is boiling water. It adds moisture to your cakes. I have tried reducing the quantity of water, and the cakes never taste as good. You may think the batter is too runny, but trust me, this method works. The second secret is cooking spray and parchment paper. This will help to keep the cake from sticking to the bottom of the pan. Spray the bottom of your pan with cooking spray (I prefer butter flavored), and then place a parchment round (the same size as the pan). Spray it again, making sure to cover the sides too. The third secret is the cooking table or surface. Make sure it is level; otherwise, your cakes will be lopsided.

VANILLA CAKE

2 cups sugar
2 cups flour
1$\frac{1}{2}$ tsp. baking soda
1$\frac{1}{2}$ tsp. baking powder
1 tsp. salt
1 tsp. vanilla extract
3 eggs
1 cup milk
$\frac{1}{4}$ cup vegetable oil
1 cup boiling water

Mix all dry ingredients well in large bowl. Add vanilla, eggs, milk, and vegetable oil to dry ingredients and mix until all ingredients are incorporated. Add boiling water and mix thoroughly. Pour into oiled 10-inch Dutch oven and bake (using baking method found in Chapter 3) for 40–45 minutes. Do not check on the cake before the time is up, or it may fall in the center.

MOIST CHOCOLATE CAKE

This cake helped my teammate and me win our first International Dutch Oven Society World Championship Cook-off in 2012. I filled the layers with a cream cheese filling mixed with strawberries, and then covered the cake in a chocolate ganache (both recipes are found in the Frostings, Ganaches, and Compotes chapter).

2 cups sugar
2 cups flour
$^3/_4$ cup unsweetened cocoa powder
$1^1/_2$ tsp. baking soda
$1^1/_2$ tsp. baking powder
1 tsp. salt
3 eggs
1 cup milk
$^1/_4$ cup vegetable oil
1 cup boiling water

Mix all dry ingredients well in large bowl. Add eggs, milk, and vegetable oil to dry ingredients and mix until all ingredients are incorporated. Add boiling water and mix thoroughly. Pour into oiled 10-inch Dutch oven and bake (using baking method found in Chapter 3) for 40–45 minutes. Do not check on the cake before the time is up, or it may fall in the center.

DELECTABLE CARROT CAKE

This cake has quickly become a favorite among my friends and family. My wife developed an allergy to nuts just recently, but she has always loved carrot cake. The traditional recipes all had nuts in them, so I came up with this one for her. This is by far one of my most requested cakes for birthdays and parties. Even the kids love it. Pair it with my Cream Cheese Frosting recipe and you will see why it is so loved.

2 cups sugar
2 cups flour
$1\frac{1}{2}$ tsp. baking soda
$1\frac{1}{2}$ tsp. baking powder
1 tsp. salt
1 tsp. cinnamon
$\frac{1}{4}$ tsp. ground nutmeg
$\frac{1}{8}$ tsp. ground cloves
3 eggs
1 cup milk
$\frac{1}{4}$ cup vegetable oil
$1\frac{1}{2}$ cups carrots, shredded
1 cup boiling water

Mix all dry ingredients well in large bowl. Add eggs, milk, vegetable oil, and carrots to dry ingredients and mix until all ingredients are incorporated. Add boiling water and mix thoroughly. Pour into oiled 10-inch Dutch oven and bake (using baking method found in Chapter 3) for 40–45 minutes. Do not check on the cake before the time is up or it may fall in the center.

TROPICAL DREAM CAKE

This cake helped my teammate and me win our second International Dutch Oven Society World Championship Cook-off in 2013, making us the first team to win back-to-back championships in the 26 years of the competition. It received a perfect score, which is virtually unheard of. Some of the comments from the judges were: "This took my breath away; it was so yummy, and as a bonus it was gorgeous outside and more impressive on the inside!" "Amazing density, unbelievable moistness, nice surprise on the inside with the checkerboard, beautiful cake." "Uniformity in layer and checkerboard pattern; nice cake texture. Enjoyed the marriage of flavors." It was also featured on a local morning news show.

In preparation for the show, I had to pre-bake four cakes, and there was not one crumb left after the show. I still chuckle when I remember how the anchors of the show decided to finish the news outside so they could make sure they got a piece of this cake before it was all gone. It was also a hit with my neighbors, due to the many test cakes prior to the competition.

It is composed of layers of two differently flavored cakes—raspberry and coconut. When I make it, I have a special tool that I use so that when it is cut it looks like a pink and white checkerboard. Topped with my Whipped Cream frosting (on page 107), it is not difficult to see why everyone loves it.

For the raspberry cake:
2 cups sugar
2 cups flour
1¹⁄₂ tsp. baking soda
1¹⁄₂ tsp. baking powder
1 tsp. salt
3 eggs
1 cup coconut milk
¹⁄₄ cup vegetable oil
5 tsp. raspberry extract
1 tsp. red food coloring
1 cup boiling water

1. Mix all dry ingredients well in large bowl. Add eggs, coconut milk, vegetable oil, raspberry extract, and food coloring to dry ingredients and mix until all ingredients are incorporated. Add boiling water and mix thoroughly. Pour into oiled 10-inch Dutch oven and bake (using baking method found in Chapter 3) for 40–45 minutes. Do not check on the cake before the time is up, or it may fall in the center.

For the coconut cake:

2 cups sugar
2 cups flour
1½ tsp. baking soda
1½ tsp. baking powder
1 tsp. salt
3 eggs
1 cup coconut milk
¼ cup vegetable oil
¼ tsp. coconut oil
1 cup boiling water

2. Mix all dry ingredients well in large bowl. Add eggs, coconut milk, vegetable oil, and coconut oil to dry ingredients and mix until all ingredients are incorporated. Add boiling water and mix thoroughly. Pour into oiled 10-inch Dutch oven and bake (using baking method found in Chapter 3) for 40–45 minutes. Do not check on the cake before the time is up, or it may fall in the center.

3. Let both cakes cool in the Dutch oven for 10–20 minutes; then, using a butter knife, go around the outer edge of the cakes to loosen them. Place a cooling rack on top of each Dutch oven (using hot gloves) and invert the cake, removing it from the Dutch oven. Let both cakes cool completely.

4. Once both cakes are completely cooled, you can cut each one into two layers. Place one layer on a serving platter or cake board, and then frost with the Whipped Cream Frosting recipe on page 107. Continue to layer cakes, alternating colors. When finished, frost the complete cake. Keep it refrigerated until you serve.

GRANDMA'S ZUCCHINI CHOCOLATE CAKE

This was one of my late Grandma Alice's recipes that she passed down to me. I was never a fan of zucchini bread, but I love this zucchini chocolate cake version. Make it for your kids and don't tell them what's in it; I guarantee they will love it.

2½ cups flour
¼ cup cocoa
1 tsp. baking soda
1 tsp. salt
½ cup butter
½ cup vegetable oil
1¾ cups sugar
2 eggs
1 tsp. vanilla extract
½ cup buttermilk
2 cups zucchini, grated
1 pkg. (6-oz.) semi-sweet chocolate chips
¾ cup walnuts, chopped

1. Sift together flour, cocoa, baking soda, and salt. Set aside. In mixing bowl, cream together butter, oil, and sugar until light and fluffy. Beat in eggs one at a time. Blend in vanilla extract. Add dry ingredients and buttermilk, alternating until mixed. Add zucchini and mix. Pour into greased 10-inch Dutch oven and sprinkle with chocolate chips and walnuts. Bake (following baking method found in Chapter 3) for 40–45 minutes.

2. Let cake cool in the Dutch oven for 10–20 minutes; then, using a butter knife, go around the outer edge of the cake to loosen it. Place a cooling rack on top of Dutch oven (using hot gloves) and invert the cake, removing it from the Dutch oven. Add frosting if desired.

RED VELVET CAKE

This cake is a hit around Christmastime, although my daughter asks for it year round. She likes that it is red but tastes like chocolate. It is very velvety and light.

2¼ cups flour
1 tsp. baking soda
½ cup cocoa
1 tsp. salt
1½ cups sugar
1½ cups vegetable oil
2 eggs
2 oz. red food coloring
1 tsp. vanilla extract
1 tsp. white vinegar
1 cup buttermilk

1. In a large bowl, combine the flour, baking soda, cocoa, and salt. In another bowl, mix the sugar and oil. Add the eggs to the sugar mixture. Blend in the food coloring, vanilla, and vinegar. Pour the liquid mixture into the flour mixture and mix. Pour into a greased 10-inch Dutch oven and bake (following baking method found in Chapter 3) for 30–40 minutes.

2. Let cake cool in the Dutch oven for 10–20 minutes. Then, using a butter knife, go around the outer edge of the cake to loosen it. Place a cooling rack on top of the Dutch oven (using hot gloves) and invert the cake, removing it from the Dutch oven. Let cool completely and frost using the Cream Cheese Frosting recipe on page 104.

PUMPKIN KAHLÚA CAKE

My teammate and I won the semi-finals for the 2012 International Dutch Oven Society World Championship Cook-off with this cake. It is a spin on the pumpkin roll my wife makes every Thanksgiving. Although I made it a four-layer cake, you can cut it to two large layers.

¾ cup flour
½ tsp. baking powder
½ tsp. baking soda
½ tsp ground cinnamon
½ tsp. ground cloves
¼ tsp. salt
3 eggs
1 cup sugar
⅔ cup 100% pure pumpkin
Heath bar topping (for decoration)

1. Mix all the ingredients, except for the Heath bar topping, together thoroughly in a large bowl. Pour into a greased 10-inch Dutch oven and bake (following the baking method found in Chapter 3) for 30–40 minutes. Repeat the recipe a second time to have enough cake for 4 layers.

2. Let the cake cool in the Dutch oven for 10–20 minutes. Then, using a butter knife, go around the outer edge of the cake to loosen it. Place a cooling rack on top of the Dutch oven (using hot gloves) and invert the cake, removing it from the Dutch oven. Let cool completely.

3. After cakes are completely cooled, cut both cakes in half to form 4 layers. Set the bottom layer on the lid or on a cake platter and spread with a layer of the Kahlúa Cream Cheese Frosting (using the recipe on page 102). Repeat with remaining layers. Chill the cake before icing the top with the Pumpkin Cream Cheese Frosting (using the recipe found on page 102). Press the Heath bar topping pieces around the sides of the cake.

RACHEALL'S DREAMY PIÑA COLADA CAKE

This was a favorite of my wife's that she used to make when she was in college. However, she used a boxed cake mix and added to it. She decided to come up with her own recipe that would allow her to make the cake from scratch. We were having dinner with some of her college friends and this recipe came up as their favorite cake. Frost it with the Piña Colada Frosting recipe found on page 102, and you will have a light, refreshing dessert that everyone will enjoy.

2 cups flour
2 tsp. baking powder
$^3/_2$ tsp. salt
1 pkg. coconut cream instant pudding mix
1 cup butter
2 cups sugar
8 egg yolks
$1^1/_2$ tsp. vanilla extract
$^1/_4$ tsp. pineapple oil
$^3/_4$ cup milk
1 cup boiling water

1. In a medium bowl, mix flour, baking powder, salt, and coconut cream pudding mix. Set aside. In a large bowl, cream together the butter and sugar until light and fluffy. Beat in the egg yolks one at a time, and then add vanilla extract and pineapple oil. Mix in the flour mixture, alternating with the milk. Mix until smooth.

2. Pour into greased 10-inch Dutch oven and bake (following baking method found in Chapter 3) for 25–30 minutes. Let cake cool in the Dutch oven for 10–20 minutes; then, using a butter knife, go around the outer edge of the cake to loosen it. Place a cooling rack on top of the Dutch oven (using hot gloves) and invert the cake, removing it from the Dutch oven. Let cool completely and frost using the Piña Colada Frosting recipe on page 102.

CHEESECAKE

Cheesecake never goes wasted in our household. This is a basic recipe that you can add fruit or other flavors to by swirling it in once the cheesecake is in the pan. We love the plain flavor with a little Raspberry Coolie (see recipe on page 104) swirled on the finished product.

For the crust:
15 graham crackers, crushed
¼ cup sugar
1 cup butter, melted

For the filling:
4 (8-oz.) pkgs. cream cheese, softened
1 cup sugar
1 tsp. vanilla extract
4 eggs

1. Put graham crackers and sugar in a food processor and turn into fine crumbs. Add butter and mix. Press into bottom of a greased 10-inch Dutch oven, covering the bottom and coming up the sides about 2 inches.

2. In a large bowl, mix cream cheese until all 4 packages are blended together. Add sugar and mix. Add vanilla extract and eggs and mix well. Pour mixture into prepared Dutch oven. Bake (using baking method found in Chapter 3) for 35–45 minutes or until a probe placed in the center comes out clean. Let cool completely before serving.

ALICE'S APPLESAUCE CAKE

After my Grandma Alice passed away, my mom sent me some of my favorite recipes from Grandma's collection. This is an oldie but a goodie. A lot of you may turn your nose up at the idea of using mayonnaise in a cake, but what is mayonnaise but eggs and oil? This cake comes out very moist and is delicious with Spiced Apples in between the layers and frosted with Cream Cheese Frosting (the recipes can be found on pages 104 and 105).

2 cups flour
$1^1/_2$ cups sugar
2 tsp. baking soda
$^1/_2$ tsp. baking powder
$^1/_4$ tsp. salt
1 tsp. cinnamon
$^1/_4$ tsp. all spice
$^1/_4$ tsp. ground nutmeg
1 tsp. vanilla extract
$^1/_2$ cup applesauce
1 cup mayonnaise
$^1/_2$ cup warm water

Mix all ingredients in a large bowl. Pour into greased 10-inch Dutch oven and bake (following baking method found in Chapter 3) for 40–45 minutes. Let cake cool in the Dutch oven for 10–20 minutes; then, using a butter knife, go around the outer edge of the cake to loosen it. Place a cooling rack on top of the Dutch oven (using hot gloves) and invert the cake, removing it from the Dutch oven. Let cake cool completely, and frost using Cream Cheese Frosting recipe on page 104.

APPLE CRUMBLE CAKE

This is a variation of a muffin recipe my wife uses. It is a delicious breakfast cake if you are in a hurry in the mornings, and it is great if you are out camping.

2 eggs
1 cup milk
1 cup butter, melted
3 cups flour
1 cup sugar
4 tsp. baking powder
1 tsp. salt
3 cups shredded apple
$^3/_4$ cup flour
$^1/_3$ cup brown sugar
$^1/_4$ cup sugar
$^1/_2$ tsp. ground nutmeg
$^1/_4$ tsp. cinnamon
$^1/_4$ tsp. ground ginger
Pinch of salt
6 Tbsp. cold butter, cut into chunks

1. Beat eggs well. Stir in milk and butter. Add flour, sugar, baking powder, and salt and mix. Add shredded apples and mix.

2. In separate bowl, mix flour, brown sugar, sugar, ground nutmeg, cinnamon, ground ginger, and salt. Cut in butter chunks until mixture is pebble sized. This is the topping.

3. Spread cake batter (which will be a little thick) into oiled 10-inch Dutch oven. Spread topping on top of batter and cover with lid. Bake using the baking method in Chapter 3 for 40–45 minutes.

BRITTANY'S CHOCOLATE CAKE

My neighbor made this cake for my family and me. It was gone within 10 minutes. I have never seen anyone eat a cake as fast as I saw my family devour this, and then they raved about it non-stop. It is chocolatey-delicious, light, and tasty.

2 cups flour
2 cups sugar
1 1/2 tsp. baking soda
1/2 tsp. salt
1 cup butter
4 Tbsp. cocoa
1 cup water
3/4 cup buttermilk (can use dry buttermilk mixed with water)
2 eggs
1 tsp. vanilla extract

1. Combine flour, sugar, baking soda, and salt and set aside. Bring to a boil the butter, cocoa, and water. Pour over dry ingredients and add buttermilk, eggs, and vanilla extract. Mix thoroughly. Bake in a 10-inch Dutch oven (using baking method found in Chapter 3) for 20–30 minutes or until a probe placed in center of the cake comes out clean.

2. Frost with Brittany's Chocolate Frosting recipe found on page 107. You'll want to frost this cake while it is still warm.

ENGLISH FRUITCAKE

This is a recipe I got from my English friend, Chris. I wanted to make him an authentic fruitcake for Christmas. For this version, we removed the alcohol and used a simple syrup to moisten it, but a true English fruitcake gets doused in brandy.

1 lb. currants
7 oz. golden raisins
7 oz. raisins
5 oz. glacé cherries (also known as maraschino or candied cherries)
3 oz. candied citrus peel
12 oz. flour
½ tsp. all spice
Pinch of cinnamon
Lemon zest of one lemon
1¼ cups butter, softened
10 oz. brown sugar
5 eggs, beaten
¼ cup orange juice, pulpless
¼ cup water

1. Mix together the currants, golden raisins, raisins, glacé cherries, and candied citrus peel until well mixed. Cover and set aside. Sift flour, all spice, and cinnamon in another bowl and set aside. In a separate bowl, cream the lemon zest, butter, and brown sugar until pale and fluffy. Gradually add the eggs, beating well after each addition. Gradually fold in flour mixture. Finally, fold in fruit mixture until evenly distributed throughout batter.

2. Oil bottom of a 10-inch Dutch oven, place parchment round in bottom, oil bottom and sides of Dutch oven, and spoon batter into it. Smooth the surface with the back of a spoon, making a slight indentation in the center. Bake using baking method for 45 minutes. Check doneness by sticking a probe in the center. If it comes out clean, the cake is done. If it doesn't, cook for another 5 minutes and check again. Let the cake cool for 10 minutes, and then invert over cooling rack, remove parchment paper from bottom, and flip right side up. Allow to completely cool.

3. In a saucepan, heat orange juice and water to make a simple syrup. Poke holes in cake and brush simple syrup mixture over cake, using all of the syrup. Wrap and turn upside down so that the top will be moist when you eat it.

LEMON CREAM CHEESE POUND CAKE

I have to admit that my wife and I are somewhat competitive in the kitchen. One day we both decided to make a dessert with lemon. I came up with this delicious lemony pound cake.

1$^{1}/_{2}$ cups butter, softened
8 oz. cream cheese, softened
3 cups sugar
6 eggs
4 Tbsp. lemon juice
Zest from one lemon
3 cups flour
1 tsp. salt

Cream together butter, cream cheese, and sugar. Add in eggs and lemon juice and mix. Add remaining ingredients and mix well. Pour into 10-inch Dutch oven. Bake (using the baking method in Chapter 3) for 60–75 minutes. It is done when a probe stuck in the center comes out clean. Make sure to replenish coals as needed to keep the temperature up.

LINDA'S CHERRY TEA CAKE

³/₄ cup vegetable oil
1¹/₂ cups sugar
1 tsp. vanilla extract
¹/₂ cup orange juice
3 eggs
3 cups flour
3 tsp. baking powder
1 (22-oz.) can cherry pie filling
1 tsp. almond extract

In a mixing bowl, mix vegetable oil and sugar. Add vanilla and orange juice. Add eggs one at a time, beating well after each one. Fold in flour and baking powder. The batter will be thick. In a separate bowl, mix pie filling and almond extract. Spread half the batter into greased 10-inch Dutch oven, and then spoon pie filling over it. Cover with remaining batter. Sprinkle sugar and cinnamon on top of batter. Bake (following baking method found in Chapter 3) for 40–50 minutes.

CRISPS, COBBLERS, AND TARTS

PEACH CRISP

I love to use fresh peaches for this recipe, but when they are out of season, frozen are just as good.

For the peaches:
5 cups peaches, sliced, fresh or frozen
$\frac{1}{2}$ cup sugar
$\frac{1}{2}$ cup brown sugar
1 tsp. cinnamon
$\frac{1}{4}$ tsp. ground nutmeg
$\frac{1}{8}$ tsp. ground cloves
Juice of 1 lime

For the topping:
1 cup quick oats
$\frac{1}{2}$ cup flour
$\frac{1}{2}$ cup sugar
$\frac{1}{2}$ tsp. cinnamon
$\frac{1}{8}$ tsp. ground nutmeg
$\frac{1}{2}$ cup butter, melted

Mix peaches, white and brown sugars, cinnamon, ground nutmeg, ground cloves, and juice of 1 lime together. Pour into a greased 10-inch Dutch oven. Mix quick oats, flour, sugar, cinnamon, and ground nutmeg. Add melted butter and mix well. Spread over peach mixture. Bake (using baking method in Chapter 3) for 45 minutes, until peaches are tender and topping has browned. Serve warm with vanilla ice cream.

PEAR TARTE TATIN

5 pears, divided
$^2/_3$ cup + 1 Tbsp. sugar
2 Tbsp. lemon juice
4 Tbsp. butter
Puff pastry
Ground nutmeg

Peel, halve, and core the pears. Put one pear aside. Cut each pear half into 3 equal wedges. Toss pears with lemon juice, nutmeg, and 1 tablespoon of sugar. In a 10-inch Dutch oven, melt butter over coals. Once melted, remove the butter from heat. Sprinkle $^2/_3$ cup of sugar evenly across the bottom of the Dutch oven. Layer the pear wedges in a single layer on top of the sprinkled sugar, using the saved pear for the center. Place back over coals and cook, without moving the pears, until the sugar is a deep caramel color. Remove from heat. Place the puff pastry over the pears and tuck the edges under. Place the lid on the Dutch oven and bake (using baking method in Chapter 3) for 25–35 minutes, until golden brown. Remove from heat and cool for a few minutes. Turn out onto a serving platter.

APPLE CRISP

My wife has been making this for years. When we moved back to Utah, it became her sister-in-law's favorite, and she requested it for her birthday every year. We like it hot out of the oven with a scoop of vanilla ice cream or, if you can find it, cinnamon ice cream.

For the fruit:
2 lb. baking apples, peeled, cored, and sliced
$^3/_4$ cup sugar
$^3/_4$ cup brown sugar
3 Tbsp. cornstarch
1 tsp. cinnamon
$^1/_4$ tsp. ground nutmeg
$^1/_4$ tsp. ground cloves
Juice of 1 lemon

For the topping:
1 cup quick oats
$^1/_2$ cup flour
$^1/_2$ cup sugar
$^1/_2$ tsp. cinnamon
$^1/_8$ tsp. ground nutmeg
$^1/_2$ cup butter, melted

1. Mix apples, sugar and brown sugar, cornstarch, cinnamon, ground nutmeg, ground cloves, and lemon juice together. Pour into a greased 10-inch Dutch oven. Mix oats, flour, sugar, cinnamon, and ground nutmeg. Add melted butter and mix well. Spread over apple mixture.

2. Bake (using baking method in Chapter 3) for 45 minutes, until apples are tender and topping has browned. Serve warm with vanilla ice cream.

BLUEBERRY CRISP

For the berries:
6 cups fresh or frozen blueberries
¼ cup sugar
1 Tbsp. cornstarch

For the topping:
1 cup quick oats
½ cup flour
½ cup sugar
½ tsp. cinnamon
⅛ tsp. ground nutmeg
½ cup butter, melted

1. Mix blueberries, sugar, and cornstarch. Pour into a greased 10-inch Dutch oven. Mix quick oats, flour, sugar, cinnamon, and ground nutmeg. Add melted butter and mix well. Spread over fruit mixture.

2. Bake (using baking method in Chapter 3) for 45 minutes, until apples are tender and topping has browned. Serve warm with vanilla ice cream.

PEACH COBBLER

For the peaches:
6 cups fresh or frozen peaches, peeled and sliced
$\frac{1}{4}$ cup sugar
$\frac{1}{4}$ cup brown sugar
1 tsp. lemon or lime juice
2 Tbsp. flour
2 tsp. cornstarch

For the topping:
2 cups flour
$\frac{3}{4}$ cup sugar
$1\frac{1}{2}$ tsp. baking powder
1 tsp. salt
Pinch of cinnamon
8 Tbsp. butter, cut in pieces
$\frac{1}{2}$ cup buttermilk

1. Combine all the ingredients for the peaches. Set aside. In a mixing bowl, mix flour, sugar, baking powder, salt, and cinnamon. Cut in butter. Add buttermilk and mix.

2. Oil a 10-inch Dutch oven and pour fruit mixture in, spreading it evenly across the bottom. Drop spoonfuls of the topping randomly over top of fruit. Using baking method (found in Chapter 3), cook for 20 minutes, or until top is golden brown. Let cool for 10 minutes before serving.

BLUEBERRY COBBLER

For the blueberries:
6 cups fresh or frozen blueberries
$^1/_4$ cup sugar
$^1/_4$ cup brown sugar
2 Tbsp. flour
2 tsp. cornstarch

For the topping:
2 cups flour
$^3/_4$ cup sugar
$1^1/_2$ tsp. baking powder
1 tsp. salt
Pinch of cinnamon
8 Tbsp. butter, cut in pieces
$^1/_2$ cup buttermilk

1. Combine all the ingredients for the blueberries. Set aside. In a mixing bowl, mix flour, sugar, baking powder, salt, and cinnamon. Cut in butter. Add buttermilk and mix.

2. Oil a 10-inch Dutch oven and pour fruit mixture in, spreading it evenly across the bottom. Drop spoonfuls of the topping randomly over top of fruit. Using baking method (found in Chapter 3), cook for 20 minutes, or until top is golden brown. Let cool for 10 minutes before serving.

APPLE FRUIT TART

1 puff pastry
$^3/_{10}$ cup sour cream
3 Tbsp. sugar
Dash of ground nutmeg
8 apples, peeled and cored
2 Tbsp. lemon juice
3 Tbsp. apricot jelly
1 Tbsp. water

1. Lightly oil 10-inch Dutch oven, and then place parchment round in the bottom and oil. Unfold puff pastry and place in Dutch oven. Roll corners to form edge. Press with fingers around the edges of remaining puff pastry to create indentations—this will hold your filling in after baking. Poke the pastry with a fork randomly. Bake for 15 minutes, until golden brown. Remove from heat. Remove pastry from Dutch oven and place on plate to cool. Pastry will be very puffy; let it cool and softly press down the center.

2. Mix together sour cream, sugar, and nutmeg and spread on cooled puff pastry. Slice apples thinly on a mandoline (to keep thickness consistent). Mix apples with lemon juice. Spiral apples around the pastry and filling. Bake in Dutch oven for 25–30 minutes. Remove from heat. Heat apricot jelly and water and brush over tart to glaze. Cool completely.

SHELL'S FRUITY TART

This is such a light and easy tart to make; you can enjoy it when your favorite fruits are in season. My wife and I like to use strawberries, raspberries, and blueberries—which is what this recipe calls for—but you can use whatever fresh fruit you want. I don't recommend using frozen fruit. The ingredient quantities in this recipe will make 2 tarts.

1 pkg. puff pastry
7 oz. marshmallow cream or fluff
4 oz. cream cheese, softened
½ pint strawberries
3 oz. raspberries
2 oz. blueberries (or use fruit of your choice)
¼ cup fruit preserves (preferably peach or apricot)
1 Tbsp. water

1. Lightly oil 10-inch Dutch oven, place parchment round in bottom, and oil. Unfold 1 puff pastry and place in Dutch oven. Roll corners to form edge. Press with fingers around the edges of remaining puff pastry to create indentations—this will hold your filling in after baking. Poke the pastry with a fork randomly. Bake for 20 minutes, until golden brown. Remove from heat. Remove pastry from Dutch oven and place on plate to cool. Pastry will be very puffy; let it cool and softly press down the center.

2. In a bowl, combine marshmallow and cream cheese until smooth. On cool pastry, place half of the mixture and spread carefully, leaving about half an inch around the edges. Slice strawberries and place a ring around pastry on filling. Place a ring of raspberries inside the strawberries, and finally place blueberries in the center.

3. Place fruit preserves and water in small Dutch oven and heat until a semi-thick syrup is formed (about 1 minute once it boils). Brush the pastry edges and the fruit with the syrup.

THREE BERRY COBBLER

This is a modified version of a friend's recipe. My wife was making it for my birthday one year, and she couldn't remember the recipe. She asked my friend's wife to send her the recipe, but when she got it, she said it didn't look right, so she changed it. Later, we found out it was correct, but in the process we found a variation that we really like too. Even my friend who gave me the original recipe likes this take on it. We love to eat it warm with vanilla ice cream. I also like to use the bag of mixed frozen berries that includes strawberries, blueberries, and raspberries, but you can use any berries that you want.

For the berries:
6 cups frozen or fresh mixed berries
¼ cup sugar
¼ cup brown sugar
2 Tbsp. flour
1 tsp. corn starch

For the topping:
2 cups flour
2 cups sugar
1 cup buttermilk
½ cup + 3 Tbsp. butter, melted
2 eggs
1 tsp. salt
1½ tsp. baking powder
Cinnamon

1. Combine all the ingredients for the berries. Set aside. In mixing bowl, mix all ingredients for topping.

2. Oil a 10-inch Dutch oven and pour fruit mixture in, spreading it evenly across the bottom. Pour topping over fruit. Using baking method (found in Chapter 3), cook for 30 minutes, or until top is golden brown. Let cool for 10 minutes before serving.

COOKIES

CHOCOLATE CHIP COOKIES

1 cup butter, softened
³/₄ cup light brown sugar
³/₄ cup sugar
2 eggs
1 tsp. vanilla extract
1 tsp. baking soda
¹/₄ tsp. salt
2¹/₄ cups flour
1 pkg. (12-oz.) chocolate chips (semi-sweet or milk chocolate)

1. Preheat 12-inch Dutch oven, following the baking method in Chapter 3.
2. Cream butter and sugars together until fluffy. Add eggs and mix well. Add vanilla extract and mix. Add dry ingredients and mix. Add chocolate chips and mix.
3. Carefully spoon the cookie dough onto the Dutch oven, leaving about 1 inch between each cookie. Replace lid and bake for 10 minutes.

BUTTERY SUGAR COOKIES

My wife has been making these sugar cookies since she was 8 years old. You can cut them out, though the shape will spread a bit. She likes to do stars or circles, and then she dips them in white and milk chocolate or frosts them with cream cheese frosting. She actually has people ask her if they can buy them because they are so addicting.

1 cup butter, softened
1 cup sugar
1 cup brown sugar
2 eggs
2 tsp. vanilla extract
$3/4$ tsp. salt
2 tsp. baking soda
2 tsp. baking powder
4 cups flour

1. Preheat 12-inch Dutch oven, following the baking method in Chapter 3.
2. Cream the butter and sugars together until fluffy. Add eggs and mix until well incorporated. Add vanilla and mix. Mix in all dry ingredients. Dough should be firm enough to roll out; if it is still sticky, add ¼ cup flour as needed.
3. Lightly flour a flat surface and a rolling pin and roll out dough to about ¼ inch thick. Cut out shapes.
4. Place cut-out cookies about 1 inch apart. Replace lid and bake for 8–12 minutes.

CUT-OUT SUGAR COOKIES

This is another recipe my wife has perfected that holds its shape well when cut into shapes. They come out thick and soft and are perfect with frosting on them.

1$^1\!/_2$ cups butter, softened
1$^1\!/_2$ cups sugar
$^1\!/_2$ cup brown sugar
4 eggs
5 cups flour
2 tsp. baking powder
1 tsp. salt

1. Preheat 12-inch Dutch oven, following the baking method in Chapter 3.

2. In a large bowl, cream together butter and sugars until smooth. Beat in eggs. Stir in dry ingredients. Cover and chill for at least 1 hour.

3. Roll out on a lightly floured surface (¼ to ½ inch thick). Cut out shapes. Place cookies 1 inch apart and bake 6–8 minutes. Cool completely and frost.

SNICKERDOODLES

Who doesn't like a good snickerdoodle? These cookies have the perfect touch of cinnamon and are nice and chewy.

1 cup butter, softened
1¹/₂ cups sugar
2 eggs
2³/₄ cups flour
2 tsp. cream of tartar
1 tsp. baking soda
¹/₄ tsp. salt
¹/₄ cup sugar
1 Tbsp. cinnamon

1. Preheat 12-inch Dutch oven, following the baking method in Chapter 3.
2. Cream butter and sugar together. Add eggs and mix. Add flour, cream of tartar, baking soda, and salt and mix well. Put dough on plastic wrap in the shape of a log and wrap. Refrigerate for 1 hour. Mix ¼ cup sugar and cinnamon together and put aside. Slice ¹/₂-inch-thick pieces of dough and roll into balls. Roll balls in the sugar and cinnamon mixture.
3. Carefully place the cookie balls onto the Dutch oven, leaving about 1 inch between each cookie. Replace lid and bake for 8–10 minutes.

OATMEAL RAISIN COOKIES

1 cup raisins
1 cup butter, softened
$1^1/_2$ cups brown sugar
2 eggs
2 cups flour
1 tsp. baking powder
1 tsp. baking soda
$^1/_2$ tsp. cinnamon
2 cups quick oats

1. Preheat 12-inch Dutch oven, following the baking method in Chapter 3.

2. Place raisins in water and let soften. Drain and rinse. Set aside. Cream butter and brown sugar until fluffy. Add eggs one at a time and mix well. In a separate bowl, mix flour, baking powder, baking soda, cinnamon, and quick oats. Add softened raisins to sugar and butter mixture. Gradually add the flour mixture. Mix well.

3. Carefully spoon the cookie dough onto the Dutch oven, leaving about 1 inch between each cookie. Replace lid and bake for 8–12 minutes.

STELLA EDMUNDS'S SHORTBREAD COOKIES

I have always loved shortbread, but I could never find a recipe I liked. Then one Christmas, my friend, who is originally from England, brought me some shortbread made with his mom's recipe. His mom was from Bradford, West Yorkshire, England, and sadly passed away in 2004. She was a great cook of traditional Yorkshire and British food, and I am honored that her son let me share this recipe. I love the mix of sugar and salt you get when you bite into these. They are definitely not for those watching their fat intake, because they use plenty of butter.

1 cup sugar
2 cups butter, softened
4 cups flour
1 heaping tsp. kosher salt

1. In a large mixing bowl, cream sugar and butter together. Add flour and salt. Mix until all the bits are pea sized. Turn out onto a floured surface and knead 5–6 minutes until combined. Butter the bottom of your 10-inch Dutch oven, drop the dough in, and press flat. Mark the surface to outline where cookies will be cut. Prick each area with a fork, pressing all the way to the bottom of the dough. Bake (using the baking method found in Chapter 3) for 35–45 minutes. Shortbread is done when a toothpick is placed in the center and comes out clean. Cool for 10 minutes in Dutch oven, and then turn out to cool completely.

PEANUT BUTTER COOKIES

I love a good peanut butter cookie. You know, the kind that is firm and buttery when you bite into it. This is my wife's recipe that she has been baking since she was a child. Make sure to pour yourself a large glass of milk with these cookies.

$^1/_2$ cup butter, softened
$^1/_2$ cup creamy peanut butter
$^1/_2$ cup sugar
$^1/_2$ cup brown sugar
1 egg
$1^1/_4$ cups flour
$^3/_4$ tsp. baking soda
$^3/_4$ tsp. baking powder
$^1/_4$ tsp. salt

1. Cream butter, peanut butter, and sugars together until fluffy. Add egg and mix well. Add dry ingredients and mix well. Make 1-inch balls out of dough. Roll dough in sugar and carefully place balls about 1 inch apart in preheated 12-inch Dutch oven. Press down with a fork, making a crisscross pattern. Replace lid and bake for 10 minutes.

CHEWY CHOCOLATE COOKIES

Not many people will turn down a chewy chocolate cookie. These are almost like brownies in cookie form.

2 cups sugar
$^{1}/_{2}$ cup butter, melted
4 (1-oz.) squares unsweetened chocolate, melted
4 eggs
2 tsp. vanilla extract
2 cups flour
2 tsp. baking powder
$^{3}/_{4}$ tsp. salt
$^{3}/_{4}$ cup confectioner's sugar

1. In large bowl, blend the sugar, butter, and chocolate. Add the eggs, one at a time, until well blended. Mix in the vanilla extract. Combine the flour, baking powder, and salt and add it gradually to chocolate mixture, mixing well after each addition. Cover and chill for 2 hours.

2. Drop the mixture by teaspoonfuls into confectioner's sugar, coating lightly, and then shape it into balls. Carefully place them on a preheated 12-inch Dutch oven (using baking method in Chapter 3). Place them about 2 inches apart and flatten them slightly. Replace the lid and bake for 12–14 minutes.

CHOCOLATE CHIP PUMPKIN COOKIES

My mother-in-law loved these cookies. They are always a treat during the fall season. They come out like little cake cookies, nice and soft.

½ cup butter, softened
1 cup brown sugar
1 egg
1 cup pumpkin
1 tsp. vanilla extract
2 cups flour
1 tsp. cinnamon
½ tsp. ground nutmeg
1 tsp. baking powder
½ tsp. baking soda
¼ tsp. salt
1 cup chocolate chips

1. In large bowl, blend sugar and butter. Add egg, pumpkin, and vanilla extract. Mix well. Combine flour, cinnamon, ground nutmeg, baking powder, baking soda, and salt; add to pumpkin mixture, mixing well after each addition. Add chocolate chips and mix.

2. Preheat 12-inch Dutch oven, using baking method in Chapter 3. Carefully place dough by the teaspoonful about 1 inch apart in Dutch oven. Replace lid and bake for 8–10 minutes.

ALMOND BISCOTTI

½ cup butter, softened
1 cup sugar
3 eggs
2 tsp. anise extract
3¼ cups flour
1 cup chopped almonds
1 Tbsp. baking powder

Cream butter and sugar until fluffy. Add eggs and beat well. Add anise extract and mix. Add flour, almonds, and baking powder. Mix and knead until smooth. Form two rolls/loaves out of dough. Place on lightly oiled 12-inch Dutch oven and bake (using baking method found in Chapter 3) for 30 minutes. Let sit for 10 minutes. Slice about 1 inch thick, place on one cut side in Dutch oven, and bake for 10 more minutes. Remove and cool.

GOOEY FUDGE BROWNIES

This recipe makes chewy, fudgy brownies that will disappear seconds after serving. If you are a chocoholic, then you will really love these. What could be better than sitting by a campfire and eating chewy brownies you just baked in a Dutch oven?

1 cup butter
4 oz. unsweetened chocolate
2 cups sugar
4 eggs
2 tsp. vanilla extract
1 1/2 cups flour

Melt the butter and chocolate over low heat, using just enough coals to melt them. Add the sugar, eggs, vanilla extract, and flour. Mix well. Pour into a greased 10-inch Dutch oven. Place coals according to the baking method found in Chapter 3. Bake for 30 minutes. Do not judge doneness by placing a probe in the center, because the center will be gooey. Remove from heat and let cool before cutting and serving.

SWEET ROLLS AND DESSERT BREADS

CINNAMON ROLLS

For years, my wife tried cinnamon roll recipes, trying to find one that would turn out a light and fluffy roll. After much searching, she adapted a recipe that she liked, and it has been a huge favorite ever since. When we first moved to Utah, she made them almost weekly. Her brother, a police officer, would bring his coworkers over on their lunch, just for a cinnamon roll. Even today, our daughter begs for them on a regular basis. A good tip to remember is to keep the milk temperature between 105 and 110 degrees; otherwise, you will kill the yeast and end up with flat rolls.

1 pkg. rapid-rise yeast
1 cup warm milk (105–110 degrees)
$^1/_2$ cup sugar
1 tsp. salt
2 eggs
$^1/_3$ cup butter, melted
4 cups flour
$1^1/_4$ cups light brown sugar
$^1/_2$ cup sugar
5 tsp. cinnamon
$^3/_4$ cup butter, softened

1. Dissolve yeast in warm milk. Add sugar, salt, and eggs and mix. Slowly mix in the melted butter. Add flour and mix well.

2. On a floured surface, knead for about 5 minutes and turn into a large ball. Place in lightly oiled bowl and cover. Let rise for 1 hour or until double in size.

3. While dough is rising, mix together light brown sugar, sugar, and cinnamon in a small bowl and set aside.

4. Once dough has risen, place onto a floured surface and roll into a ¼ inch–thick square or rectangle. Spread soft butter over the rolled-out dough and spread sugar and cinnamon mixture on top of butter. Roll into a log shape and cut into about 1-inch rolls. Place into oiled 10-inch Dutch oven and bake (using the baking method found in Chapter 3) for 25–30 minutes or until golden brown on top.

 MARTIN

BANANA BREAD

This is my wife's recipe, and she has been wowing people with it for years. In fact, when we were first dating, she promised me this delicious bread and proceeded to make it. After she pulled it out of the oven, she immediately cut a piece and put butter on it. Then, she took a bite and made the worst face—she had forgotten the sugar! The best part was that I had tasted the batter and I knew, but since we were first dating, I didn't want to say anything. When she found out, she harassed me for not telling her. Now we laugh at the memory. Whenever she makes this for anyone, I make sure to ask her if she remembered the sugar.

3 ripe bananas, creamed
1 cup sugar
$^1/_2$ cup butter, softened
2 eggs
$^1/_2$ cup milk
$2^1/_2$ cups flour
1 tsp. baking soda
$^1/_2$ tsp. baking powder
1 tsp. salt

1. Cream the butter and sugar until fluffy. Add creamed bananas and mix. Add the eggs and mix. Add the remaining ingredients and mix well. Spread into a 10-inch Dutch oven and bake (using baking method in Chapter 3) for 50–60 minutes. Bread is done when you can insert a probe in the center and it comes out clean. For an added treat, butter the top after you remove the bread from the oven.

2. Let bread cool in the Dutch oven for 10–20 minutes; then, using a butter knife, go around the outer edge of the bread to loosen it. Place a cooling rack on top of the Dutch oven (using hot gloves) and invert the bread, removing it from the Dutch oven.

PUMPKIN BREAD

This is a family favorite for fall. The colors changing and the leaves falling, along with the scent of cinnamon, nutmeg, and pumpkin permeating the air, make us all feel warm and cozy inside. The best way to eat this bread is hot out of the Dutch oven with some butter spread on it. The combination of the sweet bread and the salty butter is delectable.

1 cup sugar
$\frac{1}{2}$ cup butter, softened
2 cups pumpkin, puréed
2 eggs
$\frac{1}{2}$ cup milk
$2\frac{1}{2}$ cups flour
1 tsp. baking soda
$\frac{1}{2}$ tsp. baking powder
1 tsp. salt
$\frac{1}{4}$ tsp. ground nutmeg
3 tsp. cinnamon

1. Cream the butter and sugar until fluffy. Add pumpkin and mix well. Add the eggs and mix. Add the remaining ingredients and mix well. Spread into a 10-inch Dutch oven and bake (using baking method in Chapter 3) for 50–60 minutes. Bread is done when you can insert a probe in the center and it comes out clean. For an added treat, butter the top after you remove the bread from the oven.

2. Let bread cool in the Dutch oven for 10–20 minutes; then, using a butter knife, go around the outer edge of the bread to loosen it. Place a cooling rack on top of the Dutch oven (using hot gloves) and invert the bread, removing it from the Dutch oven.

LEMONY LEMON BREAD

You can use fresh lemons or bottled lemon juice for this recipe. My wife came up with this recipe and tried it out on her group of friends, who loved it and ate every last piece. They loved that it wasn't as dense as a lot of fruit breads. They said it was light and fluffy and didn't weigh heavy in their stomachs.

3½ cups flour
1½ cups + 3 Tbsp. sugar
4 tsp. baking powder
½ tsp. salt
2 eggs, beaten
2 cups milk
½ cup butter, melted
4 tsp. lemon zest, finely shredded
½ cup + ¼ cup lemon juice

1. In large bowl, mix flour, 1½ cups sugar, baking powder, and salt. Make a well in the center and set aside. In separate bowl, mix eggs, buttermilk, milk, butter, lemon zest, and ½ cup of lemon juice. Pour liquid mixture into well of flour mixture. Mix well.

2. Spread into a 10-inch Dutch oven and bake (using baking method in Chapter 3) for 50–55 minutes. Bread is done when you can insert a probe in the center and it comes out clean.

3. Let bread cool in the Dutch oven for 10–20 minutes; then, using a butter knife, go around the outer edge of the bread to loosen it. Place a cooling rack on top of the Dutch oven (using hot gloves) and invert the bread, removing it from the Dutch oven.

4. In a small sauce pan, mix ¼ cup of lemon juice and 3 tablespoons of sugar and bring to a boil until sugar is dissolved, making a simple syrup. Brush over finished bread.

ZUCCHINI BREAD

As a child, I found it hard to believe that a vegetable my mom forced me to eat occasionally could be turned into something delightful to eat. Since we had an abundance of zucchini from our garden, Mom made this often.

2 eggs, beaten
$1\frac{1}{3}$ cup sugar
2 tsp. vanilla extract
3 cups grated zucchini
$\frac{2}{3}$ cup butter, melted
2 tsp. baking soda
$\frac{1}{4}$ tsp. salt
3 cups flour
$\frac{1}{2}$ tsp. nutmeg
2 tsp. cinnamon

1. In a large bowl, combine the sugar, eggs, and vanilla. Mix in the grated zucchini and then the melted butter.

2. Sprinkle baking soda and salt over the mixture and stir it in. Add the flour, one cup at a time, stirring after each incorporation. Sprinkle in the cinnamon and nutmeg over the batter and mix.

3. Pour batter into oiled 10-inch Dutch oven. Bake (using baking method found in Chapter 3) for 55 minutes (check for doneness at 50 minutes), or until a probe inserted into the center comes out clean. Cool in Dutch oven for 10 minutes. Turn out onto wire racks to cool completely.

RASPBERRY BRIOCHE PUDDING

My wife saw a recipe for this, but she isn't a big fan of soggy bread and eggs, so she came up with this recipe. It's great for brunches with friends. The drizzled butter adds some decadence to it. We use 2% or 1% milk, but if you want it really creamy, use whole milk.

3 eggs
$^3/_4$ cup sugar
2 cups milk
1 cup heavy cream
1 tsp. vanilla extract
6 cups brioche (or any artisan bread that is crusty) in 1-inch cubes
1 cup fresh or frozen raspberries
$^1/_2$ cup butter, melted

1. Generously oil a 10-inch Dutch oven. In a large bowl, whisk eggs and sugar until pale and foamy. Beat in milk, cream, and vanilla extract. Scatter bread in bottom of oiled Dutch oven. Pour milk mixture over bread. Spread fruit randomly over milk and bread. Drizzle melted butter over bread.

2. Bake (using the baking method found in Chapter 3) for 1 hour with the lid on. Check to see if the center has set (using a probe). If it has, remove and let cool. If it hasn't, cook for longer, checking periodically to see if the center has set.

3. Best eaten when warm with a dollop of whipped cream.

MONKEY BREAD

This is my daughter's favorite alternative to cinnamon rolls. She likes the pockets of caramelized sugars and pudding created when baked.

24 frozen rolls, thawed
1 (3.4-oz.) pkg. butterscotch instant pudding mix
1 cup brown sugar
¼ cup sugar
3 tsp. cinnamon
1 cup butter, melted

Cut thawed rolls in half and set aside. Combine pudding mix, sugars, and cinnamon. Dip each piece of dough in butter, coat with dry mixture, and place in layers in a well-oiled 10-inch Dutch oven. If any butter is remaining, drizzle over top of dough after it is all in the Dutch oven. Cover and let rise for 1 hour, or until they are about double in size. Bake (using baking method found in Chapter 3) for 30 minutes. Let cool for 10 minutes, and then turn onto serving plate.

STRAWBERRY BREAD

2 cups of strawberries (washed & hulled)
1³/₄ cups flour
1 tsp. salt
1 tsp. baking soda
¹/₄ tsp. baking powder
2 eggs
¹/₃ cup water
³/₄ cup caster sugar
¹/₃ cup butter
¹/₂ cup chopped walnuts (optional)
Softened cream cheese (optional)
Ground cinnamon (optional)

1. Crush enough strawberries to fill one cup. Pour into a Dutch oven and heat using the braising method found in Chapter 3. Bring to boil and cook for 1 minute, stirring constantly. Remove from heat and allow to cool. Slice remaining strawberries and chill.

2. In a large bowl, combine flour, salt, baking soda, and baking powder; add eggs and water and mix well until light and fluffy. In separate bowl, beat sugar and butter together, and then add the flour mixture and mix well to blend. Stir in crushed strawberries and walnuts (optional), and spoon into 10-inch Dutch oven.

3. Bake for 1 hour or until probe placed in center comes out clean. Leave in Dutch oven to cool for 10 minutes, and then turn out on to rack to cool. Spread cream cheese on the top of the loaf, add a dusting of cinnamon, and decorate with remaining strawberries.

STICKY BUNS

1 pkg. rapid-rise yeast
1 cup warm milk (105–110 degrees)
$\frac{1}{2}$ cup sugar
1 tsp. salt
2 eggs
$\frac{1}{3}$ cup butter, melted
4 cups flour

For the filling:
1 Tbsp. brown sugar
1 Tbsp. sugar
2 tsp. cinnamon
$\frac{1}{2}$ cup butter, softened

For the sauce:
$\frac{1}{2}$ cup brown sugar
$\frac{1}{4}$ cup butter, cubed
$\frac{1}{4}$ cup corn syrup
$\frac{1}{2}$ cup pecans

1. Dissolve yeast in warm milk. Add sugar, salt, and eggs and mix. Slowly mix in the melted butter. Add flour and mix well. On a floured surface, knead for about 5 minutes and turn into a large ball. Place in lightly oiled bowl and cover. Let rise for 1 hour or until double in size.

2. While dough is rising, mix together brown sugar, sugar, and cinnamon in a small bowl and set aside. Once dough has risen, place onto a floured surface, roll into a ¼-inch-thick square or rectangle. Spread soft butter over the rolled-out dough and spread sugar and cinnamon mixture on top of butter. Roll into a log shape and cut into about 1-inch rolls. Set aside.

3. In a small Dutch oven, using the braising method in Chapter 3, combine brown sugar, cubed butter, and corn syrup. Heat until sugar is dissolved. Remove from heat and add pecans.

4. Pour syrup mixture into the bottom of a well-oiled 10-inch Dutch oven, place cut rolls on top, and bake (using the baking method found in Chapter 3) for 25–30 minutes or until golden brown on top.

5. Cool for 5 minutes and invert onto a plate.

FROSTING, GANACHES, AND COMPOTES

PIÑA COLADA FROSTING

1 (16-oz.) tub of Cool Whip or fresh whipped cream
1 pkg. coconut cream instant pudding mix
1 can crushed pineapple, drained
Shredded coconut

Empty Cool Whip/whipped cream into a large bowl; add package of pudding and crushed pineapple. Mix. Use in between layers of cake and to frost. Top with shredded coconut.

KAHLÚA CREAM CHEESE FILLING

1 (8-oz.) pkg. cream cheese, softened
1 cup butter, softened
¼ cup Kahlúa
3–5 cups powdered sugar

Cream the butter and cream cheese together. Add the Kahlúa and mix. Add enough powdered sugar to get the consistency that you want for the filling.

PUMPKIN CREAM CHEESE FROSTING

1 (8-oz.) pkg. cream cheese, softened
1 cup butter, softened
3–5 cups powdered sugar
Pumpkin pie filling

Cream the butter and cream cheese together. Add the pumpkin pie filling and mix. Add enough of the powdered sugar to get the consistency that you want for the frosting.

STRAWBERRY CREAM CHEESE FILLING

I like to use this as a filling for my chocolate cake.

1 cup butter, softened
8 oz. cream cheese, softened
8-10 strawberries, hulled and mashed
3-4 cups powdered sugar

Cream together butter and cream cheese until fluffy. Add strawberries and mix. Add powdered sugar one cup at a time until frosting is at desired consistency.

CHOCOLATE GANACHE

For this recipe, I never use chocolate chips or milk chocolate. I prefer to use Bel Noir Gold callets. Chocolate chips just never seem to melt correctly. I also do not use honey to sweeten it, but I have included it as an option in this recipe. This was what I used on my winning cake for the finals of the 2012 IDOS World Cook-off Championships.

8 oz. heavy cream
12 oz. semi-sweet chocolate (not chocolate chips)
¼ cup honey (optional)

1. In a 10-inch Dutch oven, using the braising method in Chapter 3, heat the cream, but do not let it boil. Add in about ¾ of the chocolate and stir. After the chocolate melts, remove from heat and add the remaining chocolate. Stir until melted. Adding the chocolate in this way helps to keep it from burning and to start cooling.
2. You can whip the ganache to make it spreadable and frost your cake, or you can let it cool and pour it over your cooled cake.

RASPBERRY COOLIE

This is a great topping for cheesecake. You can use other berries; just adjust the sugar to taste.

6 oz. fresh raspberries
3 Tbsp. powdered sugar
1 tsp. lemon or lime juice
2 Tbsp. water
1 tsp. cornstarch

1. In a 10-inch Dutch oven, using the braising method in Chapter 3, heat the water and raspberries. Cook until the berries are soft and have given up all of their juice.

2. With a strainer, strain the fruit into the bowl, using a spoon to push it through. Place the juice back in the Dutch oven. Add the lemon/lime juice and sugar, and stir. Adjust the sugar and juice to your taste.

3. In a cup or small bowl, mix and dissolve the cornstarch in about 2 tablespoons of water. Add to the berry mixture in the Dutch oven and stir. This will thicken it slightly. Remove from heat and chill.

CREAM CHEESE FROSTING

This is the preferred frosting for my Carrot Cake and Applesauce Cake.

1 cup butter, softened
8 oz. cream cheese, softened
1 tsp. vanilla extract
3-4 cups powdered sugar

Cream together butter and cream cheese until fluffy. Add vanilla and mix. Add powdered sugar one cup at a time until frosting is at desired consistency.

BUTTERCREAM FROSTING

This is a nice firm frosting that is good for decorating as well as just frosting.

1/2 cup shortening
1/2 cup butter, softened
4–6 cups powdered sugar
1 Tbsp. vanilla extract
2 Tbsp. milk

Cream together shortening and butter. Add sugar one cup at a time. Mix in vanilla and milk. Mix until fluffy.

SPICED APPLES

This is what I use as a filling between the layers on my Applesauce Cake.

3–4 green apples, peeled, cored, and sliced
1 tsp. cinnamon
1/4 tsp. ground nutmeg
1/8 tsp. ground cloves

In a 10-inch Dutch oven, using the braising method in Chapter 3, mix all ingredients and cook until apples are tender. Remove from heat and let cool.

BUTTER FROSTING

This is a simple, basic frosting. Be sure not to add any additional liquid, or you will need additional sugar.

1 cup butter, softened
4–6 cups powdered sugar
1 tsp. vanilla extract

Cream butter and add powdered sugar one cup at a time until desired consistency. Mix in vanilla.

STRAWBERRY COMPOTE

This compote goes great with cheesecake or any other dessert you want to try it on.

1 (16-oz.) pkg. strawberries, hulled and quartered
4 Tbsp. powdered sugar
1 Tbsp. lime juice
¼ cup water
1 tsp. cornstarch

In a Dutch oven, combine strawberries, sugar, lime juice, and water. Using the braising method found in Chapter 3, bring to a boil. Add cornstarch and boil for 1 minute. Remove from heat and cool.

BRITTANY'S CHOCOLATE FROSTING

1/2 cup butter
2 Tbsp. cocoa
1/3 cup buttermilk
2 1/2 cups powdered sugar (through sifter)

In a Dutch oven, bring butter, cocoa, and buttermilk to a boil, and then add powdered sugar and mix until smooth. Pour over warm cake.

WHIPPED CREAM FROSTING

This is the frosting I use on my Tropical Dream Cake. It is a light frosting and complements the cake well.

8 oz. cream cheese, softened
1/2 cup sugar
1 tsp. vanilla extract
2 cups heavy cream

Cream the cream cheese, sugar, and vanilla together. Add the heavy cream and whip together until the cream will hold a stiff peak.

COOKING MEASUREMENT EQUIVALENTS

Cups	Tablespoons	Fluid Ounces
⅛ cup	2 Tbsp.	1 fl. oz.
¼ cup	4 Tbsp.	2 fl. oz.
⅓ cup	5 Tbsp. + 1 tsp.	
½ cup	8 Tbsp.	4 fl. oz.
⅔ cup	10 Tbsp. + 2 tsp.	
¾ cup	12 Tbsp.	6 fl. oz.
1 cup	16 Tbsp.	8 fl. oz.

Cups	Fluid Ounces	Pints/Quarts/Gallons
1 cup	8 fl. oz.	½ pint
2 cups	16 fl. oz.	1 pint = ½ quart
3 cups	24 fl. oz.	1½ pints
4 cups	32 fl. oz.	2 pints = 1 quart
8 cups	64 fl. oz.	2 quarts = ½ gallon
16 cups	128 fl. oz.	4 quarts = 1 gallon

Other Helpful Equivalents

1 Tbsp.	3 tsp.
8 oz.	½ lb.
16 oz.	1 lb.

METRIC MEASUREMENT EQUIVALENTS

Approximate Weight Equivalents

Ounces	Pounds	Grams
4 oz.	¼ lb.	113 g
5 oz.		142 g
6 oz.		170 g
8 oz.	½ lb.	227 g
9 oz.		255 g
12 oz.	¾ lb.	340 g
16 oz.	1 lb.	454 g

Approximate Volume Equivalents

Cups	US Fluid Ounces	Milliliters
⅛ cup	1 fl. oz.	30 ml
¼ cup	2 fl. oz.	59 ml
½ cup	4 fl. oz.	118 ml
¾ cup	6 fl. oz.	177 ml
1 cup	8 fl. oz.	237 ml

Other Helpful Equivalents

½ tsp.	2½ ml
1 tsp.	5 ml
1 Tbsp.	15 ml

INDEX

AFTERWORD

When I started cooking, and the desire to learn more overcame me, I never thought that I would eventually become a two-time IDOS world champion. At the time, I wasn't even familiar with Dutch oven cooking. My desire to have good barbecue, like what I grew up around in the South, propelled me to get up the nerve to approach a local barbecue restaurant owner. T—that is his nickname—imparted his knowledge of barbecue to me and encouraged me to get into competing. My very first competition saw me take Grand Champion and refueled my competitive spirit. Who knew that I would meet my future Dutch oven partner while competing against him in barbecue? That is what I like about this community; we compete against each other, but we are also friends. When Matt Pelton asked if I would be interested in learning how to cook Dutch oven and competing with him, I was more than eager to accept. I love the Dutch oven cooking culture. People are so friendly and willing to help with new ideas and tips. Dutch oven cooking is so much more than what people realize. You can cook gourmet or you can stick to more homestyle foods, but whatever you do, I encourage you to look up your local chapter of IDOS. Find local events where you can share your recipes or even compete. These are the best places to meet new people and share ideas.

ABOUT THE AUTHOR

Doug Martin grew up in Wichita, Kansas, as the oldest of five children. His family moved to Asheville, North Carolina, when he was a junior in high school. He left for college on a soccer scholarship after graduating from high school and eventually joined the Army. He was stationed at Ft. Belvoir, Virginia, where he met and married his wife of fifteen years, Racheall. They have one beautiful daughter, Isabella, who is eleven. They moved to Utah, where Racheall was from, in 2003. A few years after moving to Utah, Doug gained his desire to learn how to cook. He began with the art of barbecue. Determined to do it right, he solicited the help of a local barbecue restaurant owner who became his mentor. His first barbecue competition saw him take Grand Champion. This only inspired him to learn more and perfect his skills. He eventually took a cake-decorating class, where he learned techniques for making his already-delicious cakes look beautiful. He met his current Dutch oven teammate, Matt Pelton, in the barbecue arena. It was there that these two formed a partnership that would make them the only Dutch oven team to win the International Dutch Oven Society World Championship two years in a row (in 2012 and 2013). This is Doug's first book. Doug travels around the West competing and teaching Dutch oven classes. He also collects, restores, and sells old cast iron he finds while antiquing.

NOTES

_____

_____

_____

_____

_____

_____

_____

_____

_____

_____

_____

_____

_____

NOTES

NOTES

_____

_____

_____

_____

_____

_____

_____

_____

_____

_____

_____

_____

_____

_____

NOTES

NOTES

NOTES